TAKE FIVE

5 Traits of Competent Kids

DL 134 · Grades 5-8

★ Above Average Ability

★ Creativity

★ Task Commitment

★ Caring

★ Courage

Written by **Kathleen Dent** & **Susan Craig**
Illustrated by **Stephanie O'Shaughnessy**

Edited by **Dianne Draze** and **Sonsie Conroy**

ISBN 1-883055-42-3

Contents

This book is dedicated to the highly competent fifth and sixth grade kids in Hamilton, Montana who helped develop this program.

A Model for Success

Ability counts for a lot in life, but, as almost everyone will tell you, it's not the only ingredient for success. How many highly capable people do you know who are not living up to their potential? When someone lacks the personal attributes that are necessary for developing all of his or her talents, the loss is not only for that individual but it is also society's loss. The bright young students sitting in our classrooms today need not only a generous helping of challenging academic content, but also a program that helps them understand their abilities and how best to develop them.

There are a number of skills and attitudes that must converge before a person can make full use of his or her natural abilities. In studying successful, productive adults, Dr. Joseph Renzulli identified three components. Using an embellished version of this model, the program outlined in this book was developed for use with academically-talented students in Montana. Students came to the program with one of the important ingredients, ability, and were given experiences that helped them understand and use these abilities in worthwhile, productive ways. With the lessons in this book, you, too, can help your students develop their full potential.

Who Is the Program For?

This nine-session program is for use with academically-talented children ages ten through fourteen. It is not meant to serve as an identification tool for gifted programs. Though it was originally designed to be used with students who participated in a gifted program, it may just as well be used with students who have not been identified as gifted but who have above-average abilities. These able students have specific

needs and concerns and can gain personal growth and insight by participation in this program.

The program focuses on five traits of competent people, which are **above average ability, creativity, task commitment, courage**, and **caring**. While participating in the nine lessons, students will complete personal evaluations and set goals in each area. Group activities are designed to foster a sense of community and personal acceptance.

Objectives

By taking part in this nine-week program, students will come to appreciate their uniqueness and realize the responsibilities of developing their potentials in a well-rounded way. Specifically, as a result of completing the activities, students will:

- be introduced to group procedures and the five traits of competent kids
- express their vision of their individual talents and abilities
- discover five personal traits that interact to produce individuals who can meet personal goals and make significant contributions to society
- take part in activities that allow them to understand these five traits and their application to their personal lives
- meet an adult who exhibits the five traits
- evaluate their strengths in relationship to the five traits and set personal goals in each area
- share information on the five traits with parents

5

Traits of Competent People

Renzulli's Three-Ring Model

Dr. Joseph Renzulli, Director of the National Research Center on the Gifted and Talented, has spent 25 years working to design and explore models to help identify and educate gifted students. He first published the "Three Ring Conception of Giftedness" (Renzulli, 1981) at a time when educators were beginning to question using only one criteria, an I.Q. score, for placement in special programs for gifted. By studying not only children but also successful, productive adults, Dr. Renzulli went beyond this one-criterion model to develop a definition of giftedness that incorporated three traits. When all three clusters of characteristics are present at the same time to a marked degree, he reasoned, the person was gifted. Through this model, educators have been able to view giftedness in a richer context. "The Three Ring Conception of Giftedness" identifies three equally-essential ingredients for creative/productive accomplishments. These are above average ability, creativity and task commitment. Renzulli states that gifted people exhibit all three of these traits and apply them to various areas of interest or expertise. The result is significant accomplishments in math, science, writing, art, music, engineering, etc.

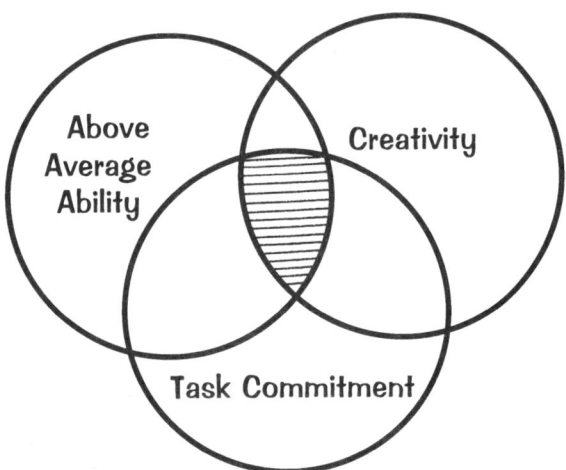

☆ Above Average Ability

Above average ability refers not just to proficiency in taking tests and getting good grades but also to aptitudes in one or more specific areas. In the school environment it has been common for teachers to identify high-ability students as those who scored in the 95th percentile or higher on standardized tests, have straight A's, or have an I.Q. of 130 or higher. Researchers studying adult populations have found that high professional accomplishments are not necessarily correlated to measured intelligence. These I.Q. test scores can only be used to screen out the students who score in the lower range. Rather, intelligence tests may serve as an indicator of potential or high ability but do not guarantee accomplishment either as a student or as an adult. Above average students tend to learn quickly and prefer high-level thinking activities.

☆ Creativity

Creativity suggests divergent and unique thinking and the ability to develop new ideas and approaches to problems. It is the ability to deal with information to find new relationships, meanings, and uses. This trait is more difficult to measure and identification is a more subjective process. Teachers discern indications of creativity in students by observing sample products and performances or looking for originality in student thinking and problem solving or in the ability to approach projects in an innovative manner. Rather than being an innate ability, many view creativity as a process of thinking or approaching tasks that can be cultivated and nurtured. Creativity is an important overlay with above average ability because without it, an individual will be very skilled at applying knowledge or implementing others' plans but will be unable to make original contributions.

☆ Task Commitment

Task commitment is the energy or motivation that is directed toward a project or goal. This personal characteristic is demonstrate by a focused manner of  accomplishing tasks. People who are task-committed have the ability to chart a course of action and to follow it to goal completion. Renzulli describes this trait as the "yeast that activates the manifestation of creative productivity." Others describe this as hard work, dedicated practice, and the intense energy gifted people can display in order to produce a desired result. This trait, coupled with ability in other areas, results usually in significant accomplishments. Without this trait, individuals may exhibit potential but never use all their abilities. They may begin projects but never see them through to a successful completion.

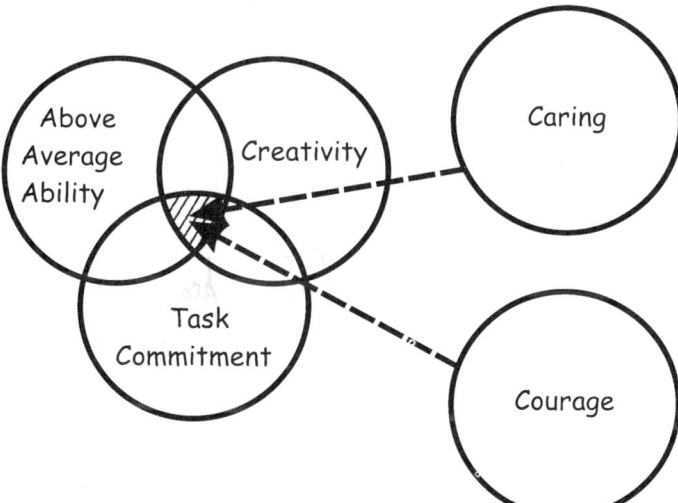

Two More Qualities

Dr. James Webb, author of *Guiding the Gifted Child,* in a keynote address entitled "Cultivating Courage, Creativity and Caring," made a case for adding two additional traits to Renzulli's "Three Ring Conception of Giftedness." By adding two additional traits to the triad, he creates a cluster of five traits of productive high-ability individuals. These traits, caring and courage, have an impact on and a relationship to the three original traits. While courage and caring are not personal characteristics only of high-ability people, there is a need to nurture these traits in high-ability children so that they will use their talents in a positive way. Only when we nurture ability, task commitment, and creativity along with caring and courage do we get individuals who will make socially responsible contributions.

Dr. Webb believes that while above average ability may be innate, courage, caring and creativity particularly need to be nurtured. The five-pronged view of giftedness is not meant to serve as an identification model, but as a holistic view through which parents and educators can help talented students learn skills that will enable them to develop their potential. By developing awareness and skills in these areas, students will be well-balanced and fully-functioning.

☆ Courage

Individuals with courage are risk-takers, people with the ability to act in spite of their fears or without assurance of success or acceptance. Without courage, individuals stick  with what is safe, and, thus, are limited in the contributions or innovations they can make in this world. Courage is needed by highly capable and creative persons in order to present their ideas and abilities to society when they know their ideas, inventions, works of art or performance may meet with criticism. Strength is required to stand behind an idea that may go against popular thought or make decisions that waver from accepted procedure. To reach their full potential, students must learn to stretch outside of their normal comfort zones. They must learn not to deny their most precious gift to society; that is, the gift of seeing the world through their own eyes and exploring their own thoughts.

☆ Caring

The final personal trait is caring, the ability to act in ways that take other people and their feelings into account. Caring actions are altruistic. The works of 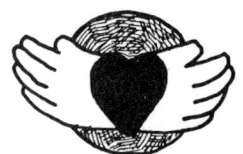 scientists, artists, philosophers, authors, scholars, engineers and leaders can be detrimental, neutral in their effect, or, with an element of caring, can provide benefits to all of society. Students can learn to observe their own behavior and assess the positive or negative effects it may have on others. This ability to act in a caring manner starts at home, in the classroom, and on the playground. As students mature, they begin to understand the cause and effect of human behavior and how it can serve society's needs in a positive way. What happens if people have the other four traits but lack caring? Then we have people who are capable and creative but act in ways that are harmful to others.

All Five Traits

When a person balances all five of these traits, he or she finds himself or herself in a powerful position to create and offer something unique and beneficial to society and, therefore, gain personal fulfillment. This does not mean that every act has to be an orchestrated product of these five factors. Instead it means that these talents and attitudes provide a backdrop to guide the behavior of highly effective and productive individuals.

As a result of taking part in this program, high-ability students will be introduced to these five personal traits so they may begin to view themselves in a holistic manner and look for ways of developing their strengths and/or remedying their weaknesses. Self-evaluation and goal-setting activities will enable them to begin the journey of self-understanding. The program instills pride in each student's individual abilities and challenges each one to use his or her talents in a responsible, caring manner.

Group Work

A group format for instruction and discussion was chosen because children are social beings, and it seemed logical that students would be comfortable meeting and discussing issues with their peers. The support students receive in a group setting is powerful. Not only is anxiety reduced when students learn that they are not alone with their issues, but a sense of belonging and support may replace feelings of loneliness and isolation.

The group format allows students to be heard by their peers as well as the group leader. The group activities are designed to allow the students to do most of the talking. Each group lesson is carefully structured and follows the theme of realizing students' potential by demonstrating the five personal traits.

The general guidelines for discussion groups are:

- The group discussions should last from 45 minutes to 1 hour, depending on the number of students and how much they have to say.
- Groups function best with about ten students.
- For all meeting, chairs should be arranged in a circle.
- For the roundtable discussions, all participants are asked to respond to a question or complete a sentence. Sharing goes from one participant to another around the circle.

The lessons in this book are designed to build a sense of trust among group members before using the group to explore individual feelings. The lessons are divided into three stages, each building on the previous one. It is important to include all stages of group development in order to insure that participants can fully benefit from the lessons.

Stage 1 - Trust Building

In this stage, students get to know each other, establish trust, learn about the goals and procedures of the group, and decide how involved they will be. This is session one.

Stage 2 - Working

At this stage the students should be acquainted with group expectations and feel valued by the group. This leads to a comfort level in which students feel they can take some risks with sharing feelings and participating in activities. In this stage students will learn about the five personal traits through discussions and exercises. Each lesson presents instructions for a group lesson, accompanying worksheets and a page of additional activities that can be used if you want to explore the topic further. This stage includes sessions two through six.

In these lessons, you may refer to the traits that are discussed as "traits of competent people" or as "qualities of personal power". Either term implies the ability to be a fully-functioning, productive individual when these five characteristics are in play.

In addition to directions for group lessons and reproducible worksheets that accompany these lessons, additional activities have been provided for each of the five traits. Several options are provided on a page that follows each lesson. These exercises are designed to be done individually and to provide opportunities for more insights into each traits. You may use these if you have time and they fit in with your program.

Stage 3 - Closure Activities

Sessions seven and eight are the closing meetings. Students are encouraged to set personal goals and apply the concepts learned to their personal lives. Sometimes it seems that just when the group gets comfortable and is in a working mode, it is time to end the group. Some students may ask if the group can continue. If the group has successfully built a spirit of community, it may be hard for some students to give it up.

Involving Parents

You may wish to send home an informational letter to inform parents of their child's participation in the group. This helps involve the parents. Hopefully they will eventually attend the parent meeting at the end of your course to learn about the five traits and to share their child's experience in the group. It is also helpful to have a meeting with the students' classroom teachers to briefly describe the goals of the program. At the end of the sessions there should be an evaluation in which teachers, parents, and students can comment on their reactions to the curriculum.

These groups are a joy to facilitate. The activities promote learning and sharing in a simple format. The meetings are fun and the discussions lively. There is never a dull group. Good luck on your journey with gifted students as they explore the possibilities of developing their talents in positive, productive ways.

(date)

Dear Parents:

    Your child has been invited to attend a nine-week course to help him/her understand and make optimum use of his/her abilities. The gifted specialist and the school counselor will conduct this course. The students will meet for a one-hour session every week to discuss five personal qualities that will enable them to develop their talents and make worthwhile contributions to society. These personal qualities are:

- *above average ability*
- *creativity*
- *task commitment*
- *courage*
- *caring*

    The goal of this program is to allow students to discuss their feelings about being identified as a gifted and talented individuals. They will also participate in activities that illustrate the five traits mentioned above and will be asked to set goals in those areas. Additionally, they will have the opportunity to learn about some adults who exhibit these characteristics.

    At the end of the program, you will be invited to share this information with your child and discuss his or her goals.

    Should you have any questions, please contact _____ at _____.

Sincerely,

- -

Please sign this permission slip and return it as soon as possible.

Child's name _____

Teacher_____

Phone _____

_____ I do give my permission for my child to participate in the Take Five program.

_____ I do not give my permission for my child to participate in the Take Five program.

Parent's signature _____ Date _____

▶ Objectives

Students will be introduced to group procedures and the five traits of competent people. They will explore and express their vision of their talents and abilities.

▶ Materials

- a sheets of art paper
- colored pencils, crayons, markers or chalk
- a large drawing of the five traits

  (You can enlarge page 12 and make a poster or make a transparency and show it on an overhead projector. This drawing should be visible at each meeting.)

▶ Procedure

Rules
- Review the rules of group discussion. Rules should include:
  - ✓ Commitment to confidentiality of the discussions
  - ✓ Respect should be shown to other members as they share with the group
  - ✓ Everyone has the right to pass once during roundtable discussions for each meeting.

Demonstrate
- Demonstrate the process of the roundtable discussion. A topic is stated and each student is allowed time to comment on the topic, starting at one point in the circle and continuing around the circle until every student has commented. Begin with the following sentence completions (or others of your choosing) to demonstrate the procedure. Each student will repeat the sentence beginning and finish the sentence. Examples are:

  "I feel happy when…
  "I feel sad when…"
  "I feel angry when…"

Diagram
- Briefly discuss the diagram of the five traits and what each element represents. Explain that the group will explore an element at each meeting and investigate how these personal qualities will allow them to make significant, positive contributions to society.

Roundtable
- Explain to the students that they were individually selected for this group. Using the roundtable discussion format, have students comment on why they feel they were selected.

Art Project
- Ask students to create a drawing that represents their own individual giftedness. It can be abstract, using lines, shapes and colors, or more literal in nature. Allow students time to work quietly, reflecting on their unique qualities.

- **Note:** *Some students will complete their drawings before the group time is over while others may want to finish it outside of class and bring it to the next meeting. When pictures are completed, it is nice to mount the drawings on a sheet of colored poster board and laminate them for use in other lessons.*

Five Traits of Competent Kids

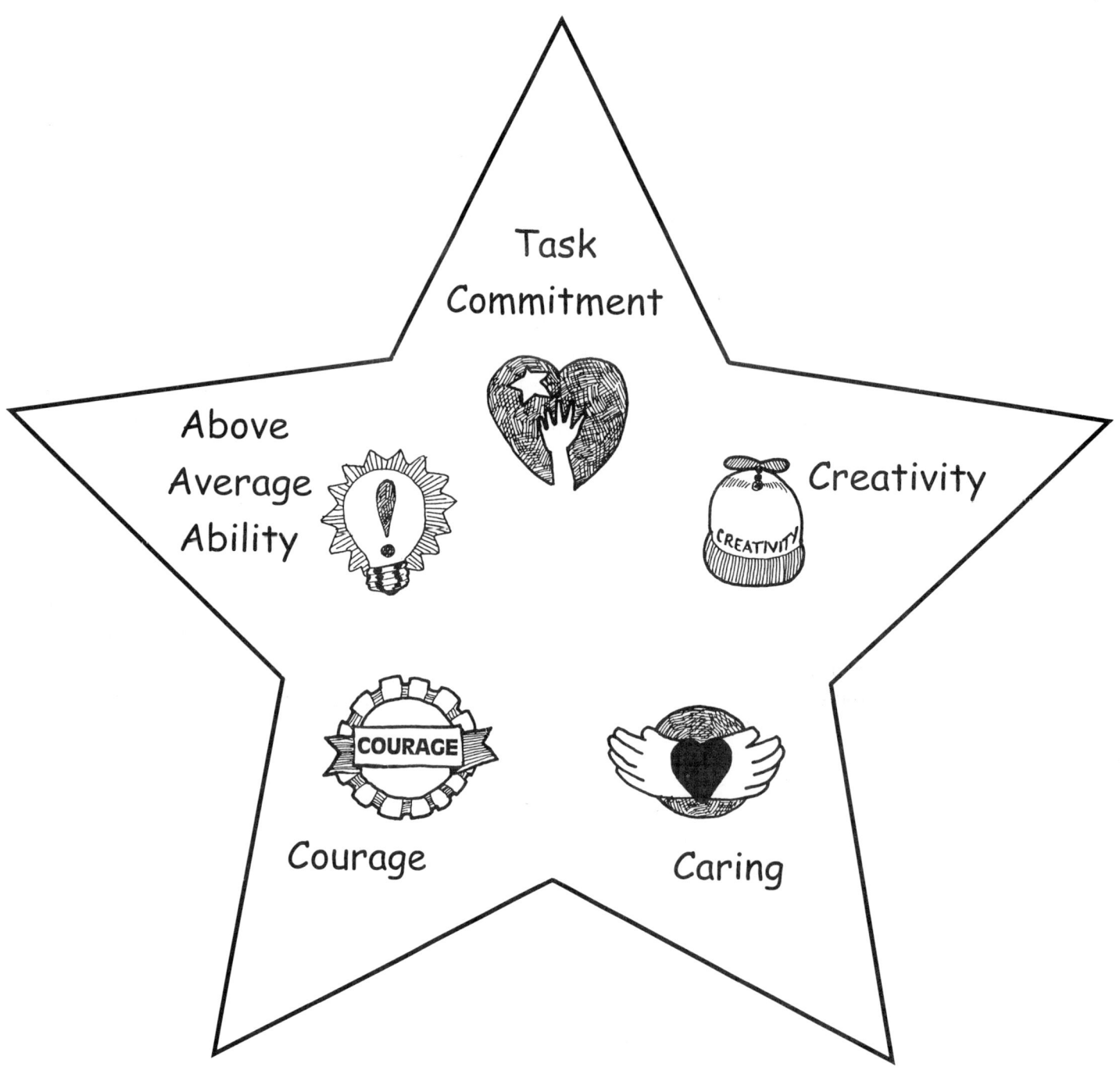

Task
Commitment

Above
Average
Ability

Creativity

Courage

Caring

Credit: Dr. James Webb as adapted from Dr. Joseph Renzulli's *Model for Giftedness Identification*

▶ Objectives

Students will explore above average ability, identify challenges associated with high ability in the regular classroom, and brainstorm strategies to meet these challenges.

▶ Materials

- a folder that will be kept by the leader and distributed at each meeting
- copy of "How Do You Measure Up?" (a listing of characteristics of students with above average ability) - page 15
- large sheets of chart paper
- artwork from Session 1 (preferably laminated and mounted on poster board)

▶ Procedure

Review Art

- Discuss the art assignment from Session 1. Give students their artwork. Using a roundtable discussion, offer students the opportunity to share their art.

- **Note:** *Neither the leader nor the group should be called upon to interpret the art. The leader should note what is created – colors, shapes, lines, forms and empty space. Comment only on what you see. Avoid interpretation or making reference to the possible content or meaning. Students may keep their art or leave it in the classroom. They may refer back to the work and may choose to share it with their parents at the parent meeting that will be held at the end of this program.*

Introduce Trait

- Explain that today's work will focus on above average ability. This is what most people associate with academic talent or high ability in the classroom. Ask students to look at the "How Do You Measure Up?" worksheet. Go around the group, asking each student to read a characteristic. As characteristics are read, have each student make a check by a characteristic if he or she feel applies to himself or herself.

Roundtable

- Have each participate respond orally to the sentence, *"One characteristic that is true about me is . . ."*

- Then go around the circle and have each participate respond orally to the sentence, *"One thing I enjoy about having above average ability is . . ."*

Discussion

- Discuss with students the fact that a person may have high abilities in several different areas, but few people have high ability in all areas. For example, a person may have high ability in music or art but be average in his or her ability to use words or numbers. Allow time to brainstorm different areas in which a person may show above average ability (math, language, singing, athletics, drawing, public speaking, science, etc.).

Roundtable

- Go around the circle and have each person complete the phrase, *"Two areas in which I feel I have above average ability are . . ."*

Discussion

- Explain that they will now look at the challenges of having these high abilities. Have them respond, one at a time, to the sentence starts, *"A frustration I have felt in the classroom is . . ."*

- Write students' responses on the chart paper. After each student expresses his or her personal frustration, it is helpful to turn to the whole group and allow other students to respond. This allows students an opportunity to recognize that other students in the group have similar feelings.

Check Off

- Then have each student go through the list of challenges and make a check by the three that are most true for him or her.

Solutions

- Once this is complete, choose the challenges with the most checks. Divide students into pairs and assign each pair one of the challenges. Allow ten minutes for students to develop as many ideas as they can to help deal with their assigned challenge. Then have them report back to the whole group. Record their ideas on chart paper and make copies of the positive solutions. Put these in each student's folder.

Close

- Close the session by having students respond to the sentence, *"One positive strategy I learned today is . . ."*

Above Average Ability

Name _____

How Do You Measure Up?

☆ Has high ability or talent in at least one particular area

☆ Is curious

☆ Learns quickly

☆ Has a good memory

☆ Has a large vocabulary

☆ Is concerned with fairness and justice

☆ Shows high motivation in subjects in which he or she is interested

☆ Is willing to consider unusual ideas

☆ Is able to think abstractly and analyze

☆ Is an independent thinker

☆ Has a sense of humor

☆ Is a risk taker

☆ Has a long attention span

☆ Foresees the consequences of things

☆ Thinks about political concerns

☆ Has a vivid imagination and produces original ideas

☆ Reads widely

☆ Is interested in a wide variety of topics

Above Average Abitites

Other activites

☆ Who do you admire? What special abilities does this person have? How does he or she use these abilities? What questions would you like to ask this person?

✳ Make twelve spaces on piece of paper. Write "I can" in each one. Finish the sentences by writing things (significant, non-trivial) that you can do well.

☆ What are your feelings about having above average ability? Write down all your ideas.

✳ How good are you at school subjects? Make a bar graph that shows how well you do in all subjects that are taught in your classroom.

✳ How would someone exhibit above average ability at your age, at ten years older than you, or as an adult? Explain your vision of exceptional ability at each stage of life.

☆ Find a want ad for a job you would like to have as an adult. What abilities would a person in this job need?

✳ What new skills would you like to develop or what subjects would you like to learn about? Make a long list.

☆ Make a collage of yourself that shows your special skills, talents and interests.

▶ Objective

Students will create imaginative pictures and share their creative ideas with the group. They will relate examples of above average ability combined with creativity.

▶ Materials

- circle of black construction paper about 6" in diameter
- white art paper
- art supplies
- copies of "Creativity Boosters" - page 19
- copies of "Mind Joggers" - page 20
- career cards - page 22
  These will be cut apart and used in several other lessons after this one.

▶ Procedure

Review
- Ask students to think back on the past week and comment on any examples they may have seen of above average ability.

Introduce Trait
- Refer to copies of page 12 (Five Traits of Competent Kids) and explain that this meeting will focus on the element of creativity. Creativity is the ability to produce original ideas, develop new patterns thoughts or products. People exhibit creativity in all areas of human endeavor (art, music, dance, writing, science, architecture, and humor are the most obvious).

Art Project
- Explain how everyone receives the same visual input. For example, three people might see a horse in a field. If they all tried to paint a picture of it, all the pictures would probably be completely different.

- For today's session, everyone will start out with the same two elements – a black construction paper circle and a pieces of white art paper. They will be given a length of time to create with and elaborate on these two elements.

- Have students go to an area of the room to work on their creations individually. After fifteen minutes the group will come back together.

Sharing
- Ask students to share their creations and explain them briefly. They should explain a little about the process that was used to decide what to create. Point out the differences and similarities in the pieces. The definition of creativity should be reviewed in order to visually identify what creativity is.

Roundtable
- Ask students to share their ideas in a roundtable format, completing the sentence, *"An example of being original and inventive in areas other than the visual arts is. . ."* or *"I use creativity when . . ."*

Combining Traits • Discuss how people use a combination of high ability and creativity to make contributions in various areas. High ability means that you can easily accumulate and understand new information. Creativity allows you to process that information to generate new and original (inventions, poetry, stories, computer programs, web sites, art, solutions for a problem, cures for a disease). Ask, *"How does high ability help creativity? How does creativity help high ability?"*

• At this point, profiles of creative people can be used to spark discussion. Provide students with books, interviews, videotapes or audiotapes.

Roundtable • Ask students to share a time when they felt they were using above average ability and creativity.

Worksheet • Give students the worksheets entitled "Creativity Boosters" and "Mind Joggers" to read through and keep in their folders as additional resources to increase their creativity.
Note: "Creativity Boosters" is adapted from "Habits of Highly Creative Writers" by Michael Bugeja and "Mind Joggers" is adapted from the SCAMPER technique created by Bob Eberle.

Career Cards • Use the career cards (page 22) to discuss how different jobs need a combination of ability in a specific field and creativity. Have students draw cards and discuss each profession in terms of these qualities.

Creativity Boosters

Here are some exercises you can do to stimulate your creativity so your writing will be more imaginative and descriptive.

1. Look up and notice things in the sky. Gaze at the stars. Notice the moon and the way its light illuminates things at night. Watch the sky and its changing colors and moods.

2. Explore nature. Look closely at a flower, an ant, a tree trunk, and a leaf. Notice the color, the texture, and the design. Ponder questions about how it grows. How does it look when it is wet? When it is dry? How does it change with the seasons? Think about the changing world of nature and notice its patterns.

3. Be kind and thoughtful to others. One selfless and considerate act inspires another. This makes you feel good about yourself and others.

4. Be a doer. Learn new things. Get involved in your community. Join clubs. Take lessons. The more involved you are in life, the more involved your mind will be as well.

5. Observe a pet closely. Sit on the grass and watch a pet play in the outdoors. Try to remember how it moves, the sounds it makes, and the expressions it seems to present on its face. Try to write a short description of what you saw and use it in the next story you write.

6. Use your five senses when you try to describe something. How does it smell? Taste? Feel? Sound? Look? The answers to these questions will generate ideas for descriptions.

Need a new idea? # Mind Joggers

Use these techniques to create original ideas and products.

✦ **Break it up** - How can you divide it into smaller parts or pieces?

✦ **Subtract** - Try to simplify it or take away some parts.

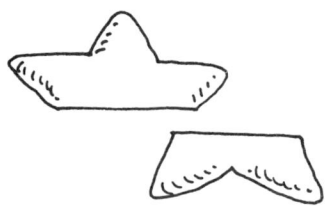

✦ **Add** - Add extra elements, functions, colors, or decorations.

✦ **Redesign** - What parts can be changed or rearranged?

✦ **Combine** - Can you bring two separate things together to make something new?

✦ **Adapt** - How else can it be used?

✦ **Substitute** - What other things could be used?

✦ **Reverse** - Can you turn it inside-out, backwards, or up-side-down?

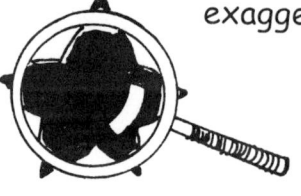

✦ **Magnify** - Make it larger, higher stronger, exaggerated.

✦ **Minimize** - Make it smaller, lower, lighter, simpler.

Adapted from the SCAMPER technique created by B. Eberle.

Creativity

Other activites

Choose a real object. How could you change it to make it appealing to a young child? a very old person? a pet? a traveler? a person your age?

Paint a picture or make a collage, using color to create a mood (like sadness, happiness, excitement, calmness, discord).

For several days, express your mood in terms of nature by writing sentences like, "I feel like the (adjective) (noun) (descriptive phrase)." Example: "I feel like the vigorous wind racing down the mountain side."

Choose a special cause that you feel strongly about. Think of creative ways that you could raise support for this cause or inform other people about it.

Choose a common article and make a long list of improvements.

How does soft sound? How does gentle look? How does nature feel? How does yellow smell?

Choose a problem in your home, school or community. Make a long list of possible solutions.

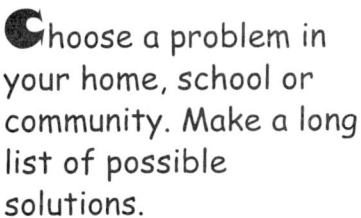

Select a favorite story and retell it in a different time period.

Cut out the career cards on this page and place them in a box. Have each student pick one career and discuss how each trait might be important for this career.

nurse	teacher	accountant
psychologist	politician	actor
astronaut	interior designer	singer
author	photographer	city planner
zoologist	minister	architect
social worker	dancer	real estate agent
computer programmer	web master	doctor
physical therapist	biologist	veterinarian
meteorologist	choreographer	genetic researcher
editor	screenplay writer	aeronautical engineer
float designer	travel agent	politician
teacher	store owner	counselor
salesperson	physicist	composer
dietician	chef	judge

22

▶ **Objectives**

Students will:

- complete a task as a group
- discuss different motivations and ways to solve roadblocks while getting the task done
- assess their motivations for staying with a task until it is complete.

▶ **Materials**

- toothpicks
- Styrofoam packing chips
- copies of "Blueprint of a Thing-a-ma-jig" (page 25)
- copies of "Personal Motivators" (page 26)

▶ **Procedure**

Introduce Trait

- Explain that today you will discuss a different personal trait, task commitment, and the class will participate in some activities that may help them learn what motivates them to complete tasks.

- Define task commitment as the motivation or drive that allows people to keep working until they complete the task or reach their goal. It is the ability or willingness to stick with something even when it is difficult.

Discussion

- Discuss the difference task commitment might make between two individuals who have equal abilities but one has task commitment and one does not. Who finishes the job? Who has a sense of satisfaction? Who gets credit for his or her accomplishments?

- Have students think to themselves whether they typically are finishers or if they usually get part way through most tasks and give up.

Simulation

- Share with the group the model of a thing-a-ma-jig. Explain that the task is to make as many thing-a-ma-jigs as they can working in a group in a ten minute period of time. They will be divided into groups and each group will be given a model, a blueprint, and materials for completing the task. Divide the students into smaller groups.

- Students will meet for five minutes to determine how they want to break down the tasks into smaller tasks so that each person in the group participates in the task completion. Each student should contribute to the finished product.

- Meet with each group separately and secretly give them separate instructions. Offer one group 50¢ for each complete thing-a-ma-jig. Tell another group that they will be graded on the quality of each product. Tell the third group that they will have to give up five minutes of recess for every Styrofoam piece or toothpick that they break. If there are more than three groups, these groups should be left without motivational instructions but visited as often as the other groups to give the appearance of equal treatment.

• Hand out a limited amount of materials to each group. This may mean that some groups run out of supplies. Do not inform them how to get more.

• Allow students ten minutes to make as many thing-a-ma-jigs as they can. At the end of the time they will count all the completed thing-a-ma-jigs and return to the circle formation.

Sharing

• Have students share their thing-a-ma-jigs and describe how the motivators worked. It may be helpful to draw a chart to compare the results.

• Talk about what things motivate students to complete real-life tasks. Discuss both positive and negative motivators. Point out the difference between intrinsic (from within) motivators and extrinsic (external) motivators.

• Consider the fact that people who accomplish great things are usually motivated by intrinsic, positive motivators. These motivators might be things like the desire to:
✓ make the world a better place
✓ do your best
✓ solve a pressing problem
✓ make a worthwhile contribution
✓ develop expertise in a field of interest.
Discuss these motivators and have students suggest other intrinsic motivators.

Worksheet

• Have students complete the "Personal Motivators" worksheet and place it in their folders..

Roundtable

• Have students each respond to the sentence starter, *"Something that keeps me from completing a task is . . ."*

• Then have them complete the sentence, *"I am most motivated by . . ."*

Combining Traits

• Ask students to give examples of how task commitment works with the qualities of above average ability and creativity to give individuals power to accomplish their goals and make worthwhile contributions.

• Have them complete the sentence, *"One time I exhibited task commitment in an area in which I have high ability was. . ."*

Career Cards

• Use the career cards (page 22) to discuss how different jobs need a combination of ability in a specific field, creativity and task commitment. Have students draw cards and discuss each profession in terms of these qualities.

Diagram Of A
Thing-a-ma-jig

Make each "thing-a-ma-jig" using this design.

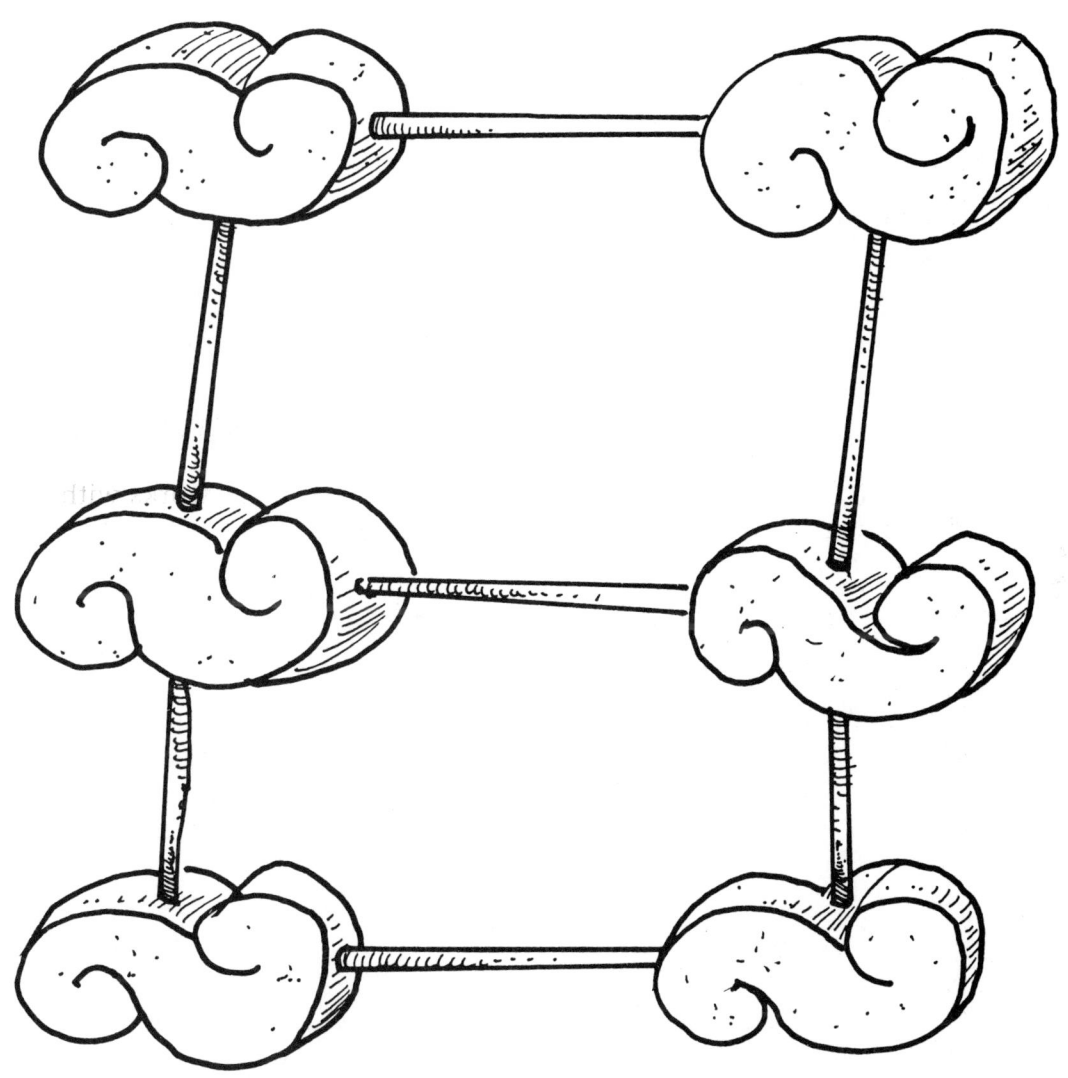

Personal Motivators

Name: _____

Positive motivators for me are...

Negative motivators for me are...

When I fail to complete a task, I feel...

When something gets in the way of working on a task, I usually...

The motivators that work best for me are...

26

Task Commitment

Other Activities

Make a list of things you can say to yourself when you feel like giving up.

Make a poster or a book cover of sayings about sticking with the task until the job is done.

What obstacles usually get in the way of you completing a goal? Make a list of how you can deal with these obstacles.

Write a letter to yourself. In the letter give yourself a pep talk about staying on task when it is difficult.

Make a list of encouraging statements and positive affirmations that make people want to keep working.

Choose several things you would like to accomplish. Tell the first two things you need to do to get started.

▶ Objective

Students will learn guidelines for courage and apply them to an experience requiring some degree of courage. They will integrate courage with the personal traits presented so far.

▶ Materials

- copies of "Guidelines for Courage" - page 30
- poster of the five traits (page 12)
- several small sheets of paper for speeches

▶ Procedure

Introduce Trait

- Refer to the poster of the five traits and explain to students that today they will be working in the area of courage. Each person will be asked to take a risk during the group meeting and to learn about guidelines for courage.

- Define courage as the strength to act in spite of your fears. It's the ability to stand up for something you believe in even if everyone else doesn't agree. It's trying something even when you're not assured of success. The risk can be mental, social, physical, or financial. People with courage are willing to take reasonable risks to accomplish something worthwhile. Stress that people should not take fool-hardy risks or risks in situations where there is no chance for success. They should take thoughtful risks, that is, risks in which they have weighed the benefits of taking the action and also the chances for success.

Roundtable

- Ask each student to tell about a time when they had to take a risk by completing the sentence, *"A time when I took a thoughtful risk was. . ."*

- Ask them to comment on how they felt before the experience and then how they felt after the experience.

- Explain that everyone has things that are more difficult and require more courage. Ask students to talk about an area that is especially difficult for them by answering the question, *"In what situations do you find it especially difficult to be courageous?"*

Speech

- Tell students that they are going to be asked to speak in front of the group for one minute on a given topic. They will be given 15 seconds to think before starting and then they must begin talking on that subject. They will be asked to stand in front of the group for the entire minute. Point out that public speaking can be very easy for some people but difficult for others.

- Ask students to rate the difficulty for them of giving a speech on a scale of one to ten where one represents very little risk involved and ten represents an extremely risky situation.

- Read the "Guidelines for Courage." Discuss briefly each point and how it might help in this situation and place the papers in their folders.

• Give students small slips of paper and ask them to write down one topic they think would make a good topic for a one-minute talk. Remind them to think of topics that would be familiar and, therefore, easy to talk about in front of the group. Collect topics, quickly reading each one to make sure it is appropriate. Have several topics prepared to replace any that are not appropriate. Put topics in a box and have students draw out a topic when it is their turn. Allow each student one minute to talk about his or her topic.

Round Table
• Facilitate a round table discussion by answering these questions:
    "I found this experience to be. . ."
    "One thing that made it easier for me was. . ."
    "One thing that made it difficult for me was. . ."

Combining Traits
• Discuss how this trait is necessary if individuals are going to make worthwhile contributions. Without it people stay with what is safe, which limits the extent of their accomplishments.

• Ask students to think of instances when they or someone else would (or did) use above average ability, creativity, task commitment and courage. One at a time have them complete the sentence, *"A time when I (or someone else)used above average ability, creativity, task commitment and courage was. . ."*

Guidelines For Courage

☀ Realize you will start at average or worse

This is sometimes tough for kids who are used to doing well, but if you are starting something new, you won't be very good at it at first.

☀ Take small steps toward your goal

Write out a few short steps to help you reach your goal. For example, if you decide you want to learn to snowboard, don't just head for the ski hill and get on the lift. Instead, learn as much as you can about the sport and take lessons from a qualified instructor. Become very familiar with your subject and make a logical start.

☀ Get support

Find four or five people who will give you help and encouragement. Invite their comments and constructive feedback. Understanding friends can encourage you to go on even when you feel like giving up. They were beginners one time, too.

☀ Keep positive, "I can" statements in your head

Don't let negative and discouraging statements run through your mind. Don't tell yourself "I know I'll make a fool of myself!" or "I'm just not any good at this." Try to keep an I-can-do-it attitude. Close your eyes and imagine yourself completing the task perfectly. Don't let the negative images fill your mind.

☀ Rejoice at any successes

Congratulate yourself at each success, no matter how small or insignificant it may seem. The big changes don't come all at once. Design a reward system for yourself. When you reach a small goal congratulate yourself. You deserve it.

Courage Other Activites

☆ **Make drawings** that show situations where people are showing courage.

☆ **Describe situations** in the classroom or on the playground where it takes courage to do the right thing.

☆ **Find statements** about courage. Make a list or a collage of these sayings. Choose the one that best applies to you.

☆ **Identify** a worthwhile cause. Tell why you could support this cause. Identify any opposition you might encounter.

☆ **Make posters** of people who have accomplished great things despite difficulties and risks.

☆ **Make and give** an award to someone in your life who you think has acted courageously.

▶ Objective
Students will discuss the effects of caring and apply the element of caring to various life situations.

▶ Materials
- copies of "The Caring Trail" worksheet (page 34) – one for each student and extras for the group activity
- copies of "Caring Stories" (pages 35-36) cut into individual stories and stored in a box

▶ Procedure

Introduce Trait
- Refer students back to the five traits. Explain that they will complete the diagram of the five traits by discussing the element of caring.
- Facilitate a roundtable discussion by having each student answer the question, *"What does having a caring attitude mean to you?"*
- After students have shared their ideas, clarify the definition, making sure to include the concepts of acting ethically and selflessly, choosing the action that will have a positive effect for other people.

Worksheet
- Explain that every day people have opportunities to show a caring attitude in many different ways, and they will have an opportunity to work in a group to come up with a variety of ways to exhibit caring in different situations.
- Break students into groups of four and give each group a copy of the "Caring Trail" worksheet. Explain that this represents a typical day in the life of a student their age. Direct them to brainstorm ways to show caring in each of the four situations. Students should take turns being recorder, so that each person is a recorder for one of the areas. Give them five minutes to complete the task.
- Ask those students who have been recorders for each area to gather as a group. For example, all the students who recorded ideas for home will get together. Give them three minutes to share the ideas for their section.
- Then have students get back into their original groups. Give them five minutes to report on the additional ideas that they discussed with people from other groups.
- Direct each individual student to reflect on the ideas that have been discussed in the groups and determine some ways that he or she can develop a caring attitude for each of the four areas. Give them five minutes to complete an individual copy of the "Caring Trail." Place these in their individual folders.

Combining Traits
- Ask for some examples of what might be the difference between using one's talent in a caring way and in a non-caring way. Reinforce the fact that a caring person thinks about other people and how they feel. They try to pay attention to how people react, and they try to help other people be successful in life. Caring people think about the effect their actions may have on others.

• Tell students that they will read descriptions of certain students and should determine how that person might use the five personal traits, particularly with caring. Have the stories (pages 35 - 36) cut apart and pass out one story to each person. Have each student read a story to the rest of the group and as the story is read, have students discuss the following things:
  ◆ identify the person's abilities
  ◆ indicate how the person could use creativity
  ◆ identify how he or she might require task commitment and courage
  ◆ suggest something each person could do that would require these qualities and would also exhibit caring.

Careers

• (optional/alternate activities) Use the career cards on page 22. Have students draw cards and discuss how using the five characteristics or traits would help someone in each career make worthwhile contributions.

• Present the following tasks and ask students to discuss what the results might be if one of the traits were missing:

✓ write a novel	✓ design a house
✓ invent a new toy	✓ find a cure for a disease
✓ design an advertisement	✓ teach school
✓ develop a website	✓ host a dinner party
✓ be PTA president	✓ be president of a business

Closure

• Tell students that they have now completed all the circles in the diagram of the five traits of competent people. Point out that when all of these characteristics are at play an individual has the ability to achieve personal excellence and contribute to society in a worthwhile way. Inform them that at the next meeting, they will hear from a member of the community who exhibits all five of these qualities. They should think of some questions to ask this person.

The Caring Trail

In what ways can you show a caring attitude during a typical day?
Record ideas for each location or time of day.

Name _____

At home

_____
_____
_____
_____
_____

Going to school

_____
_____
_____
_____
_____

At school

_____
_____
_____
_____
_____
_____
_____

After school

_____
_____
_____
_____

Caring Stories

1 Matthew is an energetic eighth grader. He whizzes through his school subjects and doesn't seem to have much homework. He spends his free time on his music. He listens to music, writes music, and plays several instruments. He also shows particular ability in mathematics.

2 Brady loves the out-of-doors. He mountain bikes competitively and in the winter is a snowboarding champion. His English teacher tells him his stories are always packed with adventure, many experiences similar to what he's actually done. Every spare minute is spent reading about extreme athletes or finding places on the map for adventure.

3 Jamal spends most of his time at the computer. He has developed a network of friends across the globe. His high school computer instructor asks him to help develop the network and mentor other students. Sometimes this irritates him because he wants to "do his own thing." He and his friends are working on developing an interactive video book.

4 Anand is a quiet seventh grader who always seems to have his nose in a book. When he speaks, he uses a large and varied vocabulary. He is well versed in many subjects but is particularly interested in insects and the toxins they use to kill their prey. He doesn't go out for sports but does like to play chess and Mah-jongg.

5 Juan is really involved in the community. Every time there is a committee formed, this junior in high school is on it. He has helped build a Habitat for Humanity home, started a food drive at the homeless shelter and volunteers at the homeless shelter once a week. His real passion is drama. He auditions for every play and usually gets a main part.

6 Lucas is a mechanical whiz. He can take apart and put together almost any car. He is the envy of the sophomore class because of his customized 1956 Chevy. In addition to cars, Frank can also repair most small appliances. He is on the honor roll in math and participates in the speech and debate club.

7 Leticia has excellent natural music ability. She loves to sing and has taken piano lessons for several years. Recently the music teacher asked her to accompany the school chorus in a concert. She really enjoys practicing and plans to begin lessons on the guitar next year.

8 Lisa is a 16-year-old high school student who loves to write stories. She has entered several short stories in a competition and received recognition for them even though they did not win a prize. Lisa is very interested in young children. When she was 8 years old her parents got a divorce and it was a very hard time for her. She would like to help children who are experiencing what she has gone through and help them learn to cope with their problems.

9 Hailey is a lover of sports. She plans to go to summer soccer camp and basketball camp. This year in middle school she was given the award for most valuable player for her basketball team and was elected by her teammates to be the captain of the team. Even with all the practices and sports events she managed to keep her grades up. She was on the honor roll last quarter.

10 Sophie loves drama and dance. She auditions for every play production in the city and at school. She has a great sense of humor. She enjoys making people laugh. At dance class she is learning to be very graceful and was given a special scholarship to go to a summer drama and dance institute at a nearby university.

11 Rosita is very interested in science. She got first place in the school science fair. Her father has a good friend who is a scientist, and she enjoys going to his house and seeing all the animals he keeps in the basement. He has a snake collection and he lets her handle the animals and tells her all about them. She enjoys lying around in her room and studying the books about animals he gave her.

12 Carmela likes people. She likes to try and persuade people to do positive things and to make the most of their lives. She likes to organize events and people. She wants to try out for cheerleader. She likes large groups of people and loves the excitement of cheering and supporting her school teams. People naturally seem to like her. Her great organizational skills help her plan things well.

Caring

✪ **Take another perspective.**
Put yourself in another person's place and tell how you think they feel.

✪ **What interests or talents**
do you have? How can you share these with other people?

What can you do
to make your community a better place? Identify people, projects, or organizations in your community that need a helping hand.

Cut out articles
from the newspaper that are examples of people acting in a caring way.

Do one act
of kindness (preferably without recognition) every day for a week. Tell how it makes you feel.

Make a list
of dos and don'ts for acting in a caring way.

▶ Objective
Students will meet and learn about an adult who exhibits the five traits in his or her life.

▶ Materials
- poster of the five traits (page 12)
- special requests from the speaker

▶ Guidelines for Inviting a Guest Speaker

Selection
- Select a member of the community who has exhibited the five traits in his or her life. All communities have many people who meet these criteria. The area of expertise is not as important as how the elements have played out in their efforts to accomplish their goals and use their abilities.

Debriefing
- Once a potential speaker has been selected and has agreed to visit the group, talk with him or her about the objectives of your class and briefly describe the types of activities completed by the students. Provide them with a copy of the traits and a copy of the goals and objectives. It is important that the speaker understand that you are requesting a personal presentation that would center on how these elements have or have not been in place for him or her. Many speakers are more comfortable talking about their subject of interest than they are talking about themselves personally.

- It is important not to try and orchestrate the presentation too much. With the information provided, each speaker should be able to individualize the ideas and present meaningful information in a unique manner.

- Ask the speaker to think about themselves at about the same age as the students in the group and to reflect back on what school was like for him or her at that time. Students always like to hear about the speaker's childhood.

▶ Procedure

Introduction
- Welcome the students and the speaker. Students should be reminded of the group rule regarding showing respect to group members and leaders. Tell them that there will be time allowed at the end of the meeting for additional questions to be answered.

- Introduce the speaker.

Presentation
- Allow the speaker about forty-five minutes for his or her presentation. The time will vary with each presenter.

- Allow students time at the end of the presentation to ask questions and make comments.

▶ Objective

Students will evaluate their strengths in relationship to the five traits and set personal goals in each area.

▶ Materials

- a deck of playing cards or numbered cards
- copies of the "Personal Strengths Graph" - page 41
- copies of "Personal Goals" - page 42

▶ Procedure

Review

- Open with a short review of the presentation given by the guest speaker. The discussion may center on some aspect of the presentation. A general beginning might be,*"Something I found to be interesting about the speaker was. . ."* or *"One way the speaker displayed the traits of competent people was when. . ."*

- Tell students that today they will take the ideas they have been learning about and apply them to their lives. They will begin by evaluating themselves in each area. Explain that most people feel more competent in one area than another. For example, creativity may seem difficult for one person when a different person may feel creativity is his or her strength. Their self-evaluations may change during different situations, subject areas, activities or stages of life.

Graph

- Ask students to look at the "Personal Strengths Graph." Using a crayon or marker, they should color each column to indicate how they feel they are generally performing at this time.

- When they finish, they can share their graphs with the group. Only students who volunteer should be asked to share.

Set Goals

- Tell students that they will take this evaluation process one step further by setting some personal goals in each of the five areas. They will **not** be asked to share their goals with the group, but the graph and goal sheets will be turned in. You will make a copy of both so you can conference with the students at some later date to check progress in reaching the goals. The graph and goals will be filed in the student's folder. Everything in the folder will be given to the student at the parent meeting.

- **Note:** *The leader's role is to encourage the students in reaching their goals throughout the year.*

Simulation

• Tell students that some aspects of our lives are similar to a card game. It sometimes seems that we are dealt a hand of cards in life, and the cards we receive are the cards we have to play out the game of life. Then deal each student one card, face down.

Note: *The cards should be arranged so each student receives a high card.*

• Have students turn their cards over for everyone to see. Tell students that this card represents the abilities they have received in life. Ask students to suggest other areas that cards might represent (health, family, geographic location).

• Give each student an additional random card for every area mentioned. Students should end up with five or six cards in their hand.

• Challenge students to look at their hands and compare them to their own lives. Ask, "How many high cards do you have? How many low cards?" Emphasize that they hold the cards but in life it is important how they play their cards. Nobody can play their hand for them. There are many people along the way who are willing to help and guide, but ultimately they are responsible for how they use their abilities and resources. Encourage students to play their hand well using the five personal traits to help them meet their goals.

Parent Meeting

• Pass out invitations to the parent meeting so students can give them to their parents. Encourage them to attend the meeting with their parents.

Personal Strengths Graph

Name _____

Color in the bars of the graph to indicate how you rate in each area at this time. Then draw a line in another color to indicate how you would like to be in each area.

CREATIVITY

COURAGE

Above Average Ability

Creativity

Task Commitment

Courage

Caring

Personal Goals

Name _____

I am setting these goals for myself in these five areas of personal power.

High Ability - The power to do something easily or well; a talent

_____
_____
_____

Creativity - The ability to generate original, inventive ideas

_____
_____
_____

Task Commitment - The motivation to follow a certain course of action to a successful completion

_____
_____
_____

Courage - The willingness to take risks or face or challenges with confidence, resolution and self-control

_____
_____
_____

Caring - To act with concern for other people

_____
_____
_____

▶ Objective

Students will share information on the five traits of competent people with parents and have the opportunity to discuss their goals.

▶ Materials

- students' folders with their work and handouts saved from the group meetings
- students' art from Sessions 1 and 3 (introduction and creativity)
- poster of the five traits (page 12)
- chart of the student's comments from Session 2 (above average ability)
- copies the evaluation forms
- light refreshments (optional)
- certificates of achievement

▶ Procedure

Have chairs or desks arranged in a circle and students' artwork displayed. Welcome everyone and explain to the parents the goals of the program following the outline below:

Roundtable	• Demonstrate to the parents the roundtable discussion procedure by using the topic "*I have fun with my family when. . .*"
Overview	• Give a brief explanation of why these students were chosen for the group.
	• Briefly explain the five traits of competent kids.
Presentations	• For above average ability share the list of ideas of how to deal with frustrations in this area.
	• For creativity have a student tell about the art exercise and show several examples.
	• For task commitment ask one of the students to tell about the activity in which they built the thing-a-ma-jig and why they were motivated to finish.
	• For courage have a student tell about his or her one-minute speech.
	• For caring show a list of ideas of how students could demonstrate caring in various ways during the day.
	• Ask a student to tell about the guest speaker or about a gifted person they learned about in the group.
	• Describe the goal-setting activity and ask students to share their goals with their parents during the social time if they feel comfortable doing so.
	• Hand out certificates.
Evaluations	• Ask students and parents to fill out the evaluation forms before leaving.

How Did It Go?

Name _____

What new ideas did you learn about how to use your talents and abilities?

_____

_____

_____

Do you think the goals you set will help you be a better student?

_____

_____

_____

What was your favorite activity?

_____

_____

_____

What other comments do you have?

_____

_____

_____

Parent Evaluation Form

Child's name _____

Your name _____

✱ During the two months your child participated in this program did your child discuss any of the topics with you at home? If so, which topics?

_____
_____
_____
_____

✱ Do you feel this was a worthwhile experience for your child?

_____
_____
_____
_____

✱ Would you like your child to participate in additional goal-setting activities?

_____
_____
_____
_____

✱ Additional comments

_____
_____
_____
_____
_____

Take Five Program

Evaluation

Teacher's Name _____

Students in the program

_____

_____

_____

_____

★ Do you think this program was a positive experience for the students in your class who participated in the group? Please explain your answer.

_____

_____

_____

★ Do you have any suggestions that might help us improve the program?

_____

_____

_____

★ Would you like your high-ability students to participate in additional goal-setting activities? _____

_____

★ Additional comments

_____

_____

_____

_____

_____

_____

_____

Optional - To be completed by students' classroom teachers.

CERTIFICATE OF ACHIEVEMENT

Presented to:

_____

Who has successfully completed the

Take Five Program

and has set goals in the areas of
Above Average Ability
Creativity
Task Commitment
Courage and
Caring.

Date _____

Signed _____

Bibliography

American Heritage Publishing Co., Inc. *The American Heritage School Dictionary*. Boston, MA: American Heritage Publishing Co., Inc. and Houghton Mifflin Company, 1972.

Brigman, Greg, and Barbara Earley. *Group Counseling for School Counselors*. Portland, ME: J. Weston Walch, 1991.

Bugeja, Michael J. "Habits of Highly Creative Writers." *Writer's Digest. February 2000: 80 (2)*

Chapman, Linda. "How to Dialogue with an Image." *Art Therapy with At Risk Children, October 7-8, 1999.*

Davis, Gary. *Teaching Values*. Cross Plains, WI: Westwood Publishing Co., 1996.

Delisle, James, and Judy Galbraith. *The Gifted Kids Survival Guide II*. Minneapolis, MN: Free Spirit Publishing Co., 1987.

Eberle, Bob. *Visual Thinking*. Buffalo, NY: DOK Publishers, 1982.

Fischer, Max W. *American History Simulations*. Huntington Beach, CA: Teacher Created Materials, Inc., 1993.

Hipp, Earl. *Fighting Invisible Tigers*. Minneapolis, MN: Free Spirit Publishing Co., 1985.

Kersey, Cynthia. *Unstoppable*. Naperville, IL: Soucebooks, Inc., 1998.

National Public Radio. *On Creativity*. New York, NY: Time Warner Trade Publishing, 1997.

Renzulli, Joseph, Sally Reis, and Linda H. Smith. *The Revolving Door Identification Model*. Mansfield, CT: Creative Learning Press, 1981.

Renzulli, Joseph. *Schools for Talent Development: A Practical Plan for Total School Improvement*, Mansfield, CT: Creative Learning Press, 1994.

Renzulli, Joseph. "What Is This Thing Called Giftedness and How Do We Develop It?" *Journal for the Education of the Gifted,* 23 (1), 3-54. 1999.

Renzulli, Joseph. *What Makes Giftedness: A Reexamination of the Gifted and Talented*. Ventura, CA: National/State Leadership Training Institute of Gifted and Talented, 1979.

Schab, Lisa M. *The Coping Skills Workbook*. King of Prussia, PA: The Center for Applied Psychology, Inc., 1996.

Schmitz, Connie C. and Judy Galbraith. *Managing the Social and Emotional Needs of the Gifted. Minneapolis, MN:* Free Spirit Publishing, 1985.

Webb, James T. "Cultivating Courage, Creativity and Caring." Presentation at the Montana Association for Gifted and Talented conference, April 2000.

Webb, James T., Elizabeth A. Meckstroth, and Stephanie Tolan. *Guiding the Gifted Child*. Scottsdale, AZ: Gifted Psychology Press, 1982.